ices

ices

sorbets, granitas, sherbets, and more

Sunil Vijayakar   **photography by Richard Jung**

RYLAND
PETERS
& SMALL
LONDON NEW YORK

First published in the
United States in 2007
by Ryland Peters & Small
519 Broadway, 5th Floor
New York, NY 10012
www.rylandpeters.com

10 9 8 7 6 5 4 3 2 1

ISBN-10: 1-84597-385-2
ISBN-13: 978-1-84597-385-8

Design and photographic art direction
Steve Painter
Commissioning Editor Julia Charles
Senior Editors Clare Double,
Lesley Malkin
Production Simon Walsh
Art Director Anne-Marie Bulat
Publishing Director Alison Starling

Home Economist Sunil Vijayakar
Prop Stylist Roisin Nield

Acknowledgments
With thanks to Magimix
(www.magimix.com) for the loan
and use of their ice cream machine.

Thanks also to Richard Jung for his
amazing photography and to Mary Wall
for assisting me in testing all the recipes
for the book.

Notes
• All spoon measurements are level unless
otherwise specified.
• All eggs are large unless otherwise
specified. Uncooked or partly cooked eggs
should not be served to the very young,
the very old, those with compromised
immune systems, or to pregnant women.

Library of Congress Cataloging-in-
Publication Data

Vijayakar, Sunil.
Ices : sorbets, granitas, sherbets, and
more / Sunil Vijayakar ; photography by
Richard Jung.
p. cm.
Includes index.
ISBN-13: 978-1-84597-385-8
1. Ice cream, ices, etc. I. Title.
TX795.V55 2007
641.8'62--dc22
2006029603

contents

everybody loves an iced treat

It is easy to make your own delicious, colorful, and healthy iced treats, experimenting with different combinations of flavors and fruits. Recipes are given for pops and other frozen novelties (fruit purées and juices mixed and frozen solid in molds), sorbets (usually a simple sugar-syrup base flavored and lightened with egg white), iced soufflés (the basic sorbet mixture but frozen in individual dishes, sometimes with gelatine for a slightly softer texture), frozen yogurts (yogurt with fruit, fruit purées, or sweeteners and frozen in molds), granitas (their texture is granular since the mixture is beaten, not churned), sherbets (like sorbets, with milk or cream added; these are made with low-fat yogurt), ices (like sorbets but without egg white, making them denser and more intensely flavored), and finally frappés and slushes (flavored fruit and sugar mixtures blitzed in the food processor, once frozen, to make them smooth but thick).

Ice cream makers aren't strictly necessary, but make the job faster and easier, and the texture slightly smoother. One with a built-in freezing unit is best – your ice cream can be ready in less than 30 minutes.

To make ices by hand, called still-freezing, set your freezer at 0°F. Cover and freeze the mixture in a freezer-proof container for ½–1 hour. Remove and beat with an electric mixer or in a food processor until the ice crystals are smooth, working quickly to minimize melting. Cover and return to the freezer, repeating 2–3 more times at 1½-hour intervals. After the final beating, allow the mixture to freeze for 2–3 hours or overnight before using. Soften very hard ices in the refrigerator for 15–20 minutes before serving.

fruit pops and other frozen novelties

Cranberry and mango make for a fabulous fruity combination. This recipe couldn't be simpler and the bars look beautiful too.

cranberry and mango bars

1¼ cups cranberry juice
1¼ cups fresh mango purée
6 rectangular molds

makes 6

Half fill the molds with the cranberry juice. Freeze for a few hours until set and top with the mango purée. Freeze again until completely frozen.

Tip: To make really good mango purée, buy the freshest, ripest, and sweetest mangoes available, skin and pit them and then blitz in a processor until smooth. If you cannot find perfectly ripe fresh mangoes, look for bagged mango pieces in the freezer case.

crushed ice sticks (golas)

These are one of the easiest, most delightful frozen treats for a hot summer's day. Use whatever fruit syrup or cordial you desire and, for adults only, these "golas" are great to dip into any liqueur of your choice.

2 cups finely crushed ice

any fruit-based syrup or cordial such as strawberry, elderflower, rose, lemon, orange, or black currant

6 wooden or bamboo skewers

makes 6

Take about ⅓ cup crushed ice in the palm of your hand and mold it around the end of a wooden or bamboo skewer, pressing tightly so the ice forms into a rough lollipop shape.

Fill small glasses with the syrup of your choice, dip the gola into the syrup, and then suck the syrup through the ice. Keep dipping until the ice is gone.

ice cube treats

Make pretty flavored decorations for your drinks or a large punch bowl by adding slices of fruit, berries, and herbs to ice cube containers. Fill with still or sparkling water and freeze until firm.

You can also freeze fruit juices in the ice cube trays and then add to long glasses of chilled soda or sparkling water.

Suggested ice cube ingredients

Fruit:

star fruit, sliced

lemons, sliced

oranges, sliced

kiwi fruit, sliced

green, red or black grapes, whole or sliced

cherries, pitted

Berries:

blackberries, whole

raspberries, whole

small strawberries, whole

blueberries, whole

Herbs:

basil leaves

mint leaves

rosemary sprigs

lemon balm leaves

The combination of strawberries and cream is a guaranteed favorite with everyone. Show them how much you care with this heart-healthy version.

iced strawberry hearts

4 cups (20 oz.) fresh or frozen strawberries, hulled and roughly chopped

6 tablespoons superfine sugar

1¼ cups low-fat vanilla yogurt

6 heart-shaped molds

makes 6

Place the strawberries and sugar in a food processor and blend until smooth. Fill the heart molds halfway up with this strawberry purée and freeze for several hours or until set. Top with the vanilla yogurt and freeze until completely frozen.

Dip the molds in hot water for a few seconds to unmold and serve immediately.

mint julep on a stick

A grown-up icy treat, perfect as a fun aperitif or perhaps a light dessert on a balmy summer's evening. To make a child-friendly version, simply leave out the bourbon.

1½ cups sugar

1 big handful fresh mint leaves, finely chopped

1 tablespoon bourbon

mint leaves, to decorate

6 frozen treat molds or small paper cups and 6 wooden treat sticks

makes 6

Place the sugar in a saucepan with 2½ cups water, heat and stir until the sugar has completely dissolved. Boil for a minute or two, then remove from the heat, and add the chopped mint leaves. Let cool completely.

When the mixture is cold, strain out the mint and add the bourbon. Pour into molds and push whole mint leaves into each one. Insert sticks and place in the freezer until frozen. To serve, dip the molds into hot water for a few seconds, and remove carefully.

mini honey kiwi pops

Kiwis are simply packed with vitamin C, and this is a really fun way to ensure you get your recommended dose.

4 ripe kiwi fruit, peeled

4–5 tablespoons honey

6 mini molds or small cupcake papers

6 sticks (optional)

makes 6

Purée the kiwi fruit in a food processor or blender and add the honey to taste—depending on the sweetness of the kiwis you may not need to use all of it. Pour into 6 mini molds or cupcake papers, insert sticks if you wish and freeze for 4–6 hours or until completely frozen.

These fabulous-looking cones are bursting at the seams with fruit, which makes them an utterly delicious and stylish way to get your five-a-day.

mixed berry and citrus cones

4 cups mixed berries such as strawberries, raspberries, blackberries, and blueberries

¾ cup confectioners' sugar

¾ cup freshly squeezed orange juice

1 tablespoon fresh lime juice

1 tablespoon fresh lemon juice

makes 6

Start by making the cones. Cut out six 6 x 12-inch lengths of waxed paper. Twist the waxed paper to form a cone shape, making sure that no hole is visible at the pointed end, and staple to secure.

Blitz the berries with the confectioners' sugar in a food processor or blender until smooth. If you wish, use a sieve to strain out all of the seeds. Put the orange juice in a small pitcher with the lime and lemon juices.

Stand the cones upright in two or three glass tumblers to support them. Spoon the berry mixture into the cone bases, then top with the juice and freeze, standing upright, for 4–6 hours or until firm. To serve, invert the cones onto a plate and gently peel off the waxed paper.

o-j pops

Commercially produced frozen fruit bars are often packed full of sugar and unhealthy additives. Give your children these homemade ones and reduce the family's dental bills.

2½ cups fresh orange juice

6 frozen treat molds and
6 wooden treat sticks

makes 6

Pour the orange juice into the treat molds. Insert the sticks and freeze for 4–6 hours or until completely solid.

When ready to serve, dip the molds in hot water for a few seconds to loosen the pops and serve immediately.

raspberry pops

Your children will delight in these ruby-colored treats. For a fun stripy effect, alternate the raspberry mixture with orange juice, freezing each layer before adding the next.

6 cups fresh or frozen raspberries

¼ cup honey

6 frozen treat molds and
6 wooden treat sticks

makes 6

Purée the raspberries in a food processor or blender. Strain through a sieve to remove the seeds, then add the honey. Pour the mixture into the treat molds, insert the sticks, and freeze for 4–6 hours or until completely solid.

When ready to serve, dip the molds in hot water for a few seconds to loosen the pops and serve immediately.

peach and plum pops

A wonderful way to capture the warmth of summer with ripe, juicy peaches and plums. Vary these pops by using any fresh fruit purée of your choice.

2 cups fresh peach purée

2 cups fresh plum purée

6 frozen treat molds with wooden sticks

makes 6

Carefully spoon a little of the peach purée into the base of 6 treat molds and top with a little of the plum mixture. Continue layering until the molds are full. Insert the sticks in the center and freeze for 4–6 hours or until firm. To serve, dip the molds in hot water for a few seconds and remove the pops.

Tip: To make the peach purée, place 1½ pounds of skinned, pitted, and chopped fresh peaches into a saucepan with ¾ cup water and sugar to taste. Bring to a boil, reduce the heat to low, and simmer gently for 4–5 minutes. Remove from the heat and process until smooth in a food processor. Make the plum purée in the same way with halved and pitted plums.

nectarine and almond sorbet

1¾ lbs. ripe nectarines, peeled, halved, and pitted

6 tablespoons granulated sugar

a few drops of pure almond extract

1 egg white

ice cream maker (optional)

makes 2½ cups, serves 4–6

This fruity ice is bursting with the flavors of a Mediterranean summer —ripe nectarines delicately flavored with a hint of almonds.

Thinly slice the nectarines and place in a saucepan with the sugar and 1¼ cups water. Bring to a boil, reduce the heat to low, cover, and simmer for 6–8 minutes or until the nectarines are just tender.

Transfer to a food processor or blender and blend until smooth. Allow to cool and then chill.

Add the almond extract, transfer to an ice cream maker, and churn until thick. If making by hand, transfer to a shallow freezer-proof container, and freeze for 4 hours or until slushy.

Whisk the egg white until just frothy, add to the ice cream maker, and continue to churn until thick enough to scoop. If making by hand, place the mixture in a processor, and whiz until softened. Add the egg white, mix well, and freeze for 4–6 hours or until firm. Serve small scoops on chilled plates.

sorbets, frozen yogurts, and iced soufflés

Almost any firm-textured, fruit-based sorbet can be frozen in treat molds to make a terrific and healthy sweet treat. Here we use plum and tangerine for this delicious sorbet.

tangerine and plum sorbet on a stick

2 lbs. ripe plums, halved, pitted, and sliced

6 tablespoons granulated sugar

freshly squeezed juice of 2 tangerines

1 small egg white

ice cream maker (optional)

6 frozen treat molds and 6 wooden treat sticks

makes 6

Place the plums, ¾ cup water, and the sugar in a saucepan and bring to a boil. Cover, reduce the heat to low, and cook for 4–5 minutes or until the sugar has dissolved and the plums are just tender. Transfer the mixture to a food processor and blend with the tangerine juice until smooth. Allow the mixture to cool, place in an ice cream maker, and churn until thick. If making the sorbet by hand, place the mixture in a shallow freezer-proof container, and freeze for 4 hours until slushy.

Whisk the egg white until frothy and add to the mixture in the ice cream maker. Continue to churn until thick enough to scoop. You can now place this mixture in any treat molds of your choice, insert a stick, and freeze until firm. If making by hand, mix the egg white into the slushy mixture, pour into molds, insert a stick, and freeze until firm.

To serve, dip the molds in hot water for 2–3 seconds, and remove carefully.

chile-lime sorbet

A twist on the classic lemon sorbet, this refreshingly tangy, deliciously smooth sorbet has a hidden kick of spiciness from the chile.

1 cup turbinado sugar

1 small fresh red chile, seeded and very finely chopped

6 large limes

1 egg white

ice cream maker (optional)

makes about 2½ cups, serves 4–6

Place the sugar, 1¼ cups water, and the chile in a saucepan over a gentle heat and stir occasionally until all the sugar has dissolved. Bring to a boil, remove from the heat, and finely grate the zest of 2 of the limes into the mixture. Set aside to cool, then chill.

Squeeze the juice from the limes and add to the syrup. Put the mixture in an ice cream maker and churn until thick. Alternatively, if making the sorbet by hand, freeze the mixture in a shallow freezer-proof container for 4 hours or until mushy.

Beat the egg white until just frothy. If using an ice cream maker, add the beaten egg white, and continue to churn until it is thick enough to scoop. If using the hand method, soften the mixture by whizzing it in a food processor, add the beaten egg white, and return the sorbet to the tub. Freeze for 4–6 hours or until firm. Serve small scoops of the sorbet in chilled glasses or cups.

blueberry and lemon sorbet

This deliciously sharp sorbet bursts with a wonderful flavor of summer. You can use mixed berries instead of the blueberries.

2 pints blueberries

¾ cup turbinado sugar

finely grated zest and freshly squeezed juice of 1 small lemon

1 egg white

glazed lemon slices and blueberries, to decorate

ice cream maker (optional)

makes about 2½ cups, serves 4–6

Place the blueberries and ⅔ cup water in a saucepan and bring to a boil. Remove from the heat and purée until smooth. Set aside to cool. Put the sugar, finely grated lemon zest and juice, and 1 cup water in a saucepan and heat gently until the sugar has dissolved. Bring to a boil, take off the heat, and transfer to a bowl. Cool and chill.

Mix the blueberries and sugar syrup. Transfer to an ice cream maker and churn until thick or, if making by hand, freeze the mixture in a shallow freezer-proof container for 4 hours or until slushy.

Whisk the egg white until just frothy and follow the instructions given in step 3 of the Chile-Lime Sorbet recipe (see left). Serve the sorbet in scoops with glazed lemon slices and blueberries to decorate.

champagne sorbet

This grown-up sorbet makes a very elegant
finale to a sophisticated meal. I have used
Champagne here but the recipe will work
equally well with any sparkling wine, such
as Italian pro secco or Spanish cava.

½ cup plus 1½ tablespoons
turbinado sugar

2⅓ cups Champagne

½ cup peach juice

ice cream maker (optional)

makes about 800 ml, serves 4–6

Place the sugar in a saucepan with ½ cup
water and heat gently until the sugar has
dissolved. Bring to a boil and remove
from the heat. Allow to cool.

Add the Champagne and peach juice to
the sugar syrup and churn in an ice cream
maker until just thick enough to scoop.
Alternatively, if making by hand place in a
shallow freezer-proof container and freeze
for 4–6 hours, whisking the partially frozen
mixture at least twice during the process.

Scoop into chilled glasses or bowls and
serve immediately.

This wonderfully speckled, pale green sorbet is made using ripe kiwis and is given a lively aromatic flavor by the addition of stem ginger. For a stronger flavor, omit the stem ginger and use a teaspoon of freshly grated ginger instead.

kiwi and stem ginger sorbet

½ cup plus 1 tablespoon granulated sugar

8 ripe kiwi fruit, peeled and roughly chopped

1 egg white, lightly beaten

2 tablespoons stem ginger, drained and finely chopped

ice cream maker (optional)

makes 2½ cups, serves 4–6

Place the sugar and 1¼ cups water in a small saucepan. Heat gently until the sugar has dissolved. Bring to a boil and remove from the heat. Allow to cool and then chill.

Place the kiwi fruit in a blender and process until smooth. Add this to the chilled syrup and stir to mix well.

If using an ice cream maker, churn the mixture until thick, add the egg white and stem ginger, and churn until firm enough to scoop. Freeze until ready to serve.

If making the sorbet by hand, pour the mixture into a shallow freezer-proof container, stir in the egg white, and allow to freeze for 3–4 hours. Place in a food processor, process until smooth, and return to the freezer, repeating this process once more. Stir in the stem ginger and freeze for 3–4 hours until firm.

Plain yogurt is flavored with maple syrup and finely chopped fresh peaches for these healthy iced treats. Vary the flavor of the yogurt and use different fruit to make your own versions of these yogurt squares.

maple-peach frozen yogurt squares

2 cups plain yogurt

⅔ cup pure maple syrup

1½ cups finely chopped fresh peaches

ice cream maker (optional)

6 square molds and 6 frozen treat sticks

makes 6

Place the yogurt in a bowl and stir in the maple syrup. Fold in the peaches and combine well.

Place the mixture in an ice cream maker and churn until firm enough to scoop. If making by hand, pour the mixture into a shallow freezer-proof container and freeze for 2 hours, whisking the partially frozen ice at least once.

Remove the mixture from the ice cream maker or container and spoon into individual square molds (approximately 2 inches square) or any other mold of your choice. Insert the sticks and freeze until firm. To serve, dip the molds in hot water for 2–3 seconds and carefully remove the squares.

Variation: Substitute finely chopped fresh pineapple for the peaches to make Tropical Pineapple Frozen Yogurt.

Colorful, tasty, and healthy, these frozen desserts make a great 'snack-attack' standby. Keep a batch of these in the freezer for unexpected young visitors.

marbled strawberry and blackberry yogurt cups

1 pint blackberries

1 pint strawberries

8 tablespoons honey

2 cups plain yogurt

6 cup molds, each about 3 inches in diameter

makes 6

Purée the blackberries and strawberries separately in a food processor until smooth. Using a sieve and spatula, strain the mixtures into separate bowls and add 2 tablespoons of the honey to each one. Stir to mix well.

Mix the yogurt with the remaining honey.

Spoon some blackberry mixture into the base of a cup mold. Carefully spoon over some yogurt mixture and then some strawberry mixture. Using a skewer, lightly marble the mixture.

Repeat with the other 5 molds and freeze for 4–6 hours or until firm. To serve, dip the molds in hot water for 2–3 seconds, remove and serve immediately.

This is a dramatic and elegant dessert which, unlike its hot relative, will not collapse on serving and can be made well in advance. Be prepared for some serious "oohs" and "aahs" from your guests.

mixed berry iced soufflés

3 cups mixed berries such as raspberries, strawberries, and blackberries

½ cup plus 2 tablespoons superfine sugar

2 egg whites

⅓ cup confectioners' sugar

2 cups Greek yogurt

6 single-portion ramekins or short paper cups

makes 6

Make 6 strips of double-thickness parchment paper to form collars around the outsides of 6 ramekins, each coming 1¼ inches above the rim. Wrap and secure each collar with a pin or tape and chill the ramekins until ready to use.

Set aside 12 of your nicest-looking berries to decorate the soufflés. Purée the remaining berries in a food processor and then press through a sieve to remove the seeds. Stir in the superfine sugar and set aside for at least 1 hour to allow the sugar to dissolve and the flavors to develop.

Whisk the egg whites until they form soft peaks, then add the confectioners' sugar and continue to whisk until glossy and firm. Beat the Greek yogurt lightly just to loosen it.

With a large spoon or spatula gently fold the berry purée, egg whites, and Greek yogurt together. Spoon into the prepared ramekins, smooth the tops, and cover with foil, taking care that the foil does not touch the tops of the soufflés. Freeze until firm.

Remove from the freezer 5–10 minutes before serving, and take off the foil and collars. Place in the refrigerator to soften a little for 5 minutes and then decorate with the reserved berries.

Who doesn't love a creamy dreamy lemon dessert?
This one ticks all the boxes and then some thanks
to the addition of cardamom. And it's low-fat to boot.

spiced citrus frozen soufflés

1 tablespoon powdered gelatine

2 egg whites

1½ cups confectioners' sugar

finely grated zest and freshly
squeezed juice of 3 lemons

½ teaspoon ground cardamom

2 cups Greek yogurt

6 single-portion ramekins
or small glasses

makes 6

Cut 6 strips of double-thickness parchment paper to form collars around the outsides of 6 ramekins, each coming 1¼ inches above the rim. Wrap and secure each collar with a straight pin or tape and chill the ramekins until ready to use.

Sprinkle the gelatine over ¼ cup cold water in a small pan and set aside for 4 minutes until the gelatine has softened. Heat very gently, stirring, without allowing to boil, until the gelatine has completely melted. Set aside.

Beat the egg whites until they form soft peaks, then add ¾ cup of the confectioners' sugar and continue to beat until glossy and firm. Fold in the lemon zest and juice and ground cardamom.

Beat the Greek yogurt and remaining confectioners' sugar lightly just to loosen, then fold in the softened gelatine.

With a large spoon or spatula gently fold together the Greek yogurt and egg white mixtures. Spoon into the prepared ramekins, smooth the tops, and cover with foil, taking care that the foil does not touch the tops of the soufflés. Freeze until firm.

Remove from the freezer 5–10 minutes before serving and take off the foil and collars. Place in the refrigerator for 5 minutes to soften a little, then serve.

granitas, sherbets, and ices

A perfectly ripe apricot is a rare and wonderful treat, however you enjoy it. This sherbet is no exception.

apricot and grape sherbet

½ cup granulated sugar

12 ripe apricots, halved and pitted

⅔ cup white grape juice

1¼ cups plain yogurt

ice cream maker

makes 2½ cups, serves 4–6

Make a syrup by gently heating ⅔ cup water and the sugar in a pan, stirring to dissolve the sugar. Add the apricots and simmer for 5 minutes. Remove from the heat and let cool.

Once cooled, transfer the apricots and syrup to a food processor or blender and process until smooth. Press through a sieve and stir in the grape juice and yogurt.

Transfer the mixture to an ice cream maker and churn until thick. Spoon into a plastic container and freeze for 4–5 hours or until firm.

Blood oranges have been cultivated in Sicily since ancient times. An unassuming peel, tinged with purple, conceals a flesh ranging from rose to almost black: pure drama, especially in this festive ice.

blood orange ice

8 large blood oranges

½ cup plus 1 tablespoon granulated sugar

ice cream maker

makes about 2½ cups, serves 4–6

Wash the oranges in hot water to remove any waxy coating.

Put the sugar and ¾ cup water in a saucepan. Using a zester or vegetable peeler, pare thin strips of the zest from 1 of the oranges, and add to the sugar and water. Heat gently, stirring until the sugar has completely dissolved. Bring to a boil and then remove from the heat and let cool. Strain out the zest, juice the oranges, and add the juice to the syrup.

Transfer the mixture to an ice cream maker and churn until it holds its shape. Spoon into a shallow plastic container and freeze for 3 hours. Remove from the freezer, beat for a minute or two, and return to the freezer for a couple of hours or until firm enough to scoop.

Tip: If you are unable to find fresh blood oranges, use 2¼ cups of bottled blood-orange juice instead.

espresso granita

A refreshing "pick-me-up," great after a lazy summer lunch. The cardamom lends it an exotic hint of mystery. If you have nothing planned for the afternoon, try adding a tablespoon or two of coffee liqueur.

5 tablespoons good-quality espresso or strong filter coffee

1 quart boiling water

¾ cup granulated sugar

¼ teaspoon ground cardamom

2 tablespoons Kahlúa or other coffee liqueur (optional)

makes about 2½ cups, serves 4–6

Prepare your coffee in a French press or filter machine. If using a French press, let stand for 5 minutes after adding the water before plunging. Pour the coffee into a large shallow plastic container and add the sugar. Stir until completely dissolved, then add the cardamom and Kahlúa, if using, and let the mixture cool.

Cover and freeze for 2 hours or until the coffee mixture is starting to look mushy.

Break up the ice crystals with a fork and finely mash them. Return the granita to the freezer for another 2 hours, mashing every 30 minutes, until the ice forms fine, even crystals. After the final mashing return to the freezer for at least an hour before serving.

green tea and mint granita

A sophisticated and refreshing take on iced tea—just looking at the minty green color will make you feel cooler!

¾ cup granulated sugar

3 green tea teabags

1 handful fresh mint leaves

makes about 2½ cups, serves 4–6

Put the sugar and 2½ cups water in a saucepan, heat gently, and stir until dissolved. Bring to a boil and remove from the heat. Add the teabags and let infuse for 5 minutes. Meanwhile, finely chop the mint leaves.

Remove the teabags from the pan and allow the syrup to cool completely. When it is cool, add the finely chopped mint leaves and stir through.

Pour the mixture into a large, shallow plastic container, and freeze for 2 hours. Remove from the freezer and with a fork mash up any crystals that have formed. Return to the freezer for another 2 hours and repeat the mashing. Freeze for at least another hour before serving.

pomegranate granita

This once hard-to-find fruit, a native of the Middle East, has a thick waxy skin enclosing hundreds of jewellike ruby seeds. The juice is hailed as a great antioxidant and is now widely available in many supermarkets.

1 cup granulated sugar

2½ cups pomegranate juice

pomegranate seeds,
to decorate (optional)

makes about 2½ cups, serves 4–6

In a large shallow plastic container, stir the sugar into the juice until dissolved.

Cover and freeze for 2 hours or until the mixture is starting to look mushy.

Using a fork, break up the ice crystals and finely mash them. Return the granita to the freezer for another 2 hours, mashing every 30 minutes, until the ice forms fine, even crystals. After the final mashing return to the freezer for at least an hour before serving. Decorate with the fresh pomegranate seeds, if using.

orange and lemon granita

Zing zing zing! Your taste buds won't know what's hit them. Zesty doesn't even begin to describe this wide-awake, citrus assault on the senses.

½ cup plus 1 tablespoon sugar

6 oranges

2 lemons

makes about 2½ cups, serves 4–6

Put the sugar and ¾ cup water into a saucepan. Using a zester or vegetable peeler, pare thin strips of zest from 1 orange and 1 lemon and add them to the sugar and water. Heat gently, stirring until the sugar has completely dissolved. Bring to a boil and then remove from the heat and let cool. When cold, strain the liquid into a large shallow plastic container.

Juice the fruit and stir into the syrup to combine. Freeze for 2 hours. Remove from the freezer and with a fork mash up any crystals that have formed. Return to the freezer for another 2 hours and repeat the mashing process. Freeze again for at least 1 more hour before serving.

spicy plum sherbet

Curl up and take comfort from summer's parting gift. This cold-yet-warming spicy plum sherbet is perfect for those early autumn days when plums still abound yet there is a decided nip in the air.

½ cup plus 2 tablespoons granulated sugar

1 cinnamon stick

4 cloves

1 inch fresh ginger, peeled and sliced

12 ripe plums, halved and pitted

1½ cups low-fat plain yogurt

ice cream maker

makes about 2½ cups, serves 4–6

Put the sugar, cinnamon, cloves, ginger, and 6 tablespoons water in a saucepan and heat gently, stirring to dissolve the sugar. Add the plums and simmer for 5 minutes. Remove from the heat and let cool.

Once cool, discard the cinnamon and cloves, transfer the plums and syrup to a food processor or blender, and process until smooth. Press through a sieve into a bowl and stir in the yogurt.

Transfer the mixture to an ice cream maker and churn until thick. Spoon into a plastic container and freeze for 4–5 hours or until firm.

raspberry sherbet

Pink, creamy, and luscious—this sherbet sounds far naughtier than it actually is! Fresh berries and fat-free yogurt make for a delightfully low-fat treat.

½ cup plus 2 tablespoons granulated sugar

2½ cups raspberries

1½ cups fat-free yogurt

ice cream maker

makes about 2½ cups, serves 4–6

Gently heat the sugar and 6 tablespoons water in a saucepan, stirring to dissolve the sugar. Bring to a boil and remove from the heat.

Purée the raspberries in a food processor or blender. Press through a sieve to remove the seeds. Stir into the cold syrup and chill until very cold.

Add the yogurt to the purée and whisk until smooth.

Transfer the mixture to an ice cream maker and churn until thick. Spoon into a plastic container and freeze for 4–5 hours or until firm.

This would be the perfect ending to an Eastern-inspired meal. Star anise and mandarin oranges are natural partners as both originate in China. The star anise not only adds a wonderful licorice flavor, it also looks stunning and makes for a very stylish decoration.

star anise and mandarin orange granita

¾ cup sugar

6 whole star anise

20 fresh mandarin oranges (tangerines)

makes about 2½ cups, serves 4–6

Put the sugar and ¾ cup plus 2 tablespoons water in a saucepan and heat gently, stirring until the sugar has completely dissolved. Add the star anise and simmer without stirring for 2 minutes. Remove from the heat and let cool.

Cut a slice off the top and bottom of each mandarin, then slice away the peel and pith. Chop the flesh roughly and process in a food processor until almost smooth. Press the resulting pulp through a sieve into a large shallow plastic container. Strain the syrup into the same container, reserving the star anise. Mix well, cover, and freeze for 2 hours or until the mixture is starting to look mushy.

Using a fork, break up and finely mash the ice crystals. Return the granita to the freezer for another 2 hours, mashing every 30 minutes, until the ice forms fine, even crystals. After the final mashing return to the freezer for at least an hour before serving. Decorate with the reserved star anise if you wish.

On a sticky summer day there is nothing better than sinking your teeth into a slice of refrigerator-cold watermelon. Nothing, that is, except this vivid granita with a hint of lime.

watermelon granita

¾ cup granulated sugar

4 lbs. watermelon

finely grated zest and freshly squeezed juice of 1 lime

makes about 2½ cups, serves 4–6

Put the sugar and ⅔ cup water in a pan and slowly bring to a boil, stirring to dissolve the sugar. Once boiled, remove from the heat, and let cool.

Scoop out the flesh from the watermelon and discard the seeds. Blitz briefly in a food processor until smooth and then strain through a sieve into a large shallow plastic container. Add the syrup, lime zest and lime juice, and mix well.

Freeze for 2 hours. Remove from the freezer and with a fork mash any crystals that have formed. Return to the freezer for another 2 hours and repeat the mashing process. Freeze for at least 1 more hour before serving.

frappés, slushes, and frozen drinks

This tropical, thick, and cooling sorbet-drink evokes memories of golden beaches, azure seas, and swaying palm trees. For a child-friendly version, omit the rum.

iced piña colada

2 cups chopped ripe fresh pineapple

6 tablespoons superfine sugar

¾ cup coconut milk

4 tablespoons white rum

ice cream maker

makes about 2 cups, serves 2

Stir the pineapple with the sugar to mix well. Let stand for 10 minutes at room temperature to allow the sugar to dissolve into the chopped pineapple. Place all the ingredients in an ice cream maker and churn until softly slushy. Pour into chilled glasses and serve immediately.

frozen strawberry fruit soda

Scoops of sorbet, served in a froth of sparkling zesty soda, would make a perfect treat for many children. This refreshing soda has great adult appeal too.

Strawberry sorbet

3 cups strawberries,
roughly chopped

¾ cup granulated sugar

freshly squeezed juice of 1 lime

ice cream maker

To serve

¾ cup raspberries

¾ cup chilled sparkling lemonade
(or other soda of your choice)

makes about 2½ cups, serves 2

Make the sorbet by placing all the ingredients in a saucepan with 1¼ cups water and bringing to a boil. Reduce the heat to low and gently simmer for 3–4 minutes. Remove from the heat and when cool process in a blender until smooth. Churn the mixture in an ice cream maker until thick and then transfer to a shallow freezer-proof container or ice cube trays and freeze until firm.

Place 2 tall glasses in the freezer to chill for 10 minutes. Place 3 scoops or cubes of the sorbet into the base of each glass. Add the raspberries and top up each glass with the sparkling lemonade.

frozen apple and cinnamon spritzer

The fresh flavors of apple juice infused with cinnamon make a lovely icy drink with a fizzy topping of sparkling wine. For children, replace the sparkling wine with ginger ale.

1¼ cups clear apple juice

2 cinnamon sticks

about ½ cup chilled sparkling white wine

makes about 1¼ cups, serves 2

Place the apple juice and cinnamon in a small saucepan and bring to a boil. Remove from the heat and allow to cool. Discard the cinnamon sticks. Transfer to a shallow freezer-proof container and freeze for about 2 hours or until a layer of ice crystals has formed around the edges. Mash with a fork and return to the freezer for another 2–3 hours or until almost solid.

Spoon the apple ice into a food processor and briefly process until very slightly slushy. Transfer to 2 chilled glasses and top with the chilled sparkling wine.

Here pears are combined with rich-flavored plums to make a smooth and beautifully colored slush with a gentle hint of rosemary. Choose sweet pears and plums and always use the ripest fruit for natural sweetness.

pear and plum slush

1 pear (approximately 6 oz.)

14 oz. plums, halved and pitted

¾ cup granulated sugar

1 small sprig of rosemary

ice cream maker (optional)

makes about 2½ cups, serves 4–6

Peel, core, and roughly chop the pear. Put in a saucepan with the plums, sugar, rosemary, and 2 cups water. Place over a gentle heat and bring to a boil. Reduce the heat to low and cook gently for 10–12 minutes. Discard the rosemary and transfer the mixture to a blender. Process until smooth and sieve.

Churn the mixture in an ice cream maker until just soft and slushy. If making the slush by hand, place the mixture in a shallow freezer-proof container and freeze for 6–8 hours or until firm. Remove, transfer to a food processor, and process until softly slushy. Serve in chilled glasses.

pink grapefruit and basil frappé

Frappés fall somewhere between granitas and slushes and can be eaten with a spoon or sucked with a thick straw (watch out for brain freeze!). Refreshing and not too sweet, this is a delicate pale pink color flecked with basil, and flavored with its subtle aniseed tones.

1 cup plus 2 tablespoons granulated sugar

4 large pink grapefruit

1 handful basil leaves, finely sliced

makes about 2½ cups, serves 4–6

Put the sugar and 1¼ cups water in a pan with the zest of 1 grapefruit. Heat gently, stirring to dissolve the sugar. Simmer for 5 minutes. Let cool.

Juice all the grapefruits. Strain the cooled syrup and add the juice and the basil.

Stir well and freeze for 3 hours in a large shallow container or ice cube trays.

Before serving, transfer to a blender and crush until smooth.

rhubarb and ginger frappé

The ginger and rhubarb weave magic together in this bittersweet, spicy frappé, which is sure to delight all rhubarb lovers.

1½ lbs. rhubarb, chopped

½ cup granulated sugar

1 inch fresh ginger, peeled and finely grated

makes about 2½ cups, serves 4–6

Put the rhubarb in a pan with the sugar, ginger, and 6 tablespoons water. Cover and cook over a medium heat for 4–5 minutes. Remove from the heat and let cool.

Once cold, transfer to a food processor or blender, and purée. Freeze for 3 hours in a large shallow container or ice cube trays.

Before serving, transfer to a blender and crush until smooth.

index

conversion chart

Weights and measures have been rounded up
or down slightly to make measuring easier.

Volume equivalents:

American	Metric	Imperial
1 teaspoon	5 ml	
1 tablespoon	15 ml	
¼ cup	60 ml	2 fl.oz.
⅓ cup	75 ml	2½ fl.oz.
½ cup	125 ml	4 fl.oz.
⅔ cup	150 ml	5 fl.oz. (¼ pint)
¾ cup	175 ml	6 fl.oz.
1 cup	250 ml	8 fl.oz.

Weight equivalents:

Imperial	Metric
1 oz.	30 g
2 oz.	55 g
3 oz.	85 g
3½ oz.	100 g
4 oz.	115 g
5 oz.	140 g
6 oz.	175 g
8 oz. (½ lb.)	225 g
9 oz.	250 g
10 oz.	280 g
11½ oz.	325 g
12 oz.	350 g
13 oz.	375 g
14 oz.	400 g
15 oz.	425 g
16 oz. (1 lb.)	450 g

Measurements:

Inches	Cm
¼ inch	5 mm
½ inch	1 cm
¾ inch	1.5 cm
1 inch	2.5 cm
2 inches	5 cm
3 inches	7 cm
4 inches	10 cm
5 inches	12 cm
6 inches	15 cm
7 inches	18 cm
8 inches	20 cm
9 inches	23 cm
10 inches	25 cm
11 inches	28 cm
12 inches	30 cm

Freezer temperature:

–18°C	0°F